Sleeping with the Devil

By

Antonio and Marsha Gonzales

Copyright © 2023

Antonio and Marsha Gonzales

All rights reserved.

ISBN: 9798386812171

Published by Liberty River Industries
2229 Village Lake Drive
Charlotte, NC 28212

The Christian Standard Bible. Copyright © 2017 by Holman Bible Publishers. Used by permission. Christian Standard Bible®, and CSB® are federally registered trademarks of Holman Bible Publishers, all rights reserved.

New Revised Standard Version Bible Copyright © 1989 by the Division of Christian Education of the National Council of the Churches of Christ in the United States of America

Scripture quotations marked (NLT) are taken from the Holy Bible, New Living Translation, copyright ©1996, 2004, 2015 by Tyndale House Foundation. Used by permission of Tyndale House Publishers, Carol Stream, Illinois 60188. All rights reserved.

Scripture quotations marked (NIV) are taken from the Holy Bible, New International Version®, NIV®. Copyright © 1973, 1978, 1984, 2011 by Biblica, Inc.™ Used by permission of Zondervan. All rights reserved worldwide. www.zondervan.comThe "NIV" and "New International Version" are trademarks registered in the United States Patent and Trademark Office by Biblica, Inc.™

Scripture taken from the New King James Version®. Copyright © 1982 by Thomas Nelson. Used by permission. All rights reserved.

"Scripture quotations are from The ESV® Bible (The Holy Bible, English Standard Version®), copyright © 2001 by Crossway, a publishing ministry of Good News Publishers. Used by permission. All rights reserved."

Bible text from the Good News Translation (GNT) is not to be reproduced in copies or otherwise by any means except as permitted in writing by American Bible Society, 101 North Independence Mall East, FL 8, Philadelphia, PA 19106 -2155 (www.americanBible.org).

Scripture taken from the Common English Bible®, CEB® Copyright © 2010, 2011 by Common English Bible.™ Used by permission. All rights reserved worldwide.

Printed in the United States of America. All rights reserved under International Copyright Law. Contents and/or cover may not be reproduced in whole or in part in any form without the express written consent of the publisher.

LIBERTY RIVER

Antonio and Marsha Gonzales

DEDICATION

Our family and others (meaning friends, strangers, professional people, church, and social media) have seen this marriage on display. God spoke to me, saying, "I'm going to use this marriage for My glory." With all the pain and heartache, I couldn't understand such a statement. Truly we give You all the glory.

We want to thank every pastor who took the time, even the pastors who told me to leave him. I mean, I wrestled with this. I would hear their voices saying, "God wouldn't give you someone to hurt you," yet we were hurting each other. Sin is sin. No sin is greater than the next.

One day I had an open vision and was sitting in the Garden of Gethsemane. I asked God what I should do. He said, "Must this cup pass you?" I knew my answer.

We would also like to thank sister one, who never took sides. At least if she did, she never displayed that toward me, but people tend to do what everybody else does, so they want to get mad at them. She brought to her mom's attention that his actions were wrong and that I had every right to put her son in jail for touching me.

I wouldn't say I liked fighting, only if I had to, and I promised myself I would never be like my mom. She always had my dad bleeding, and that did something to me. Even though it was never explained to me, it affected me. I never wanted to hurt people like that.

My husband always lied to me. I was proclaimed as the toxic one, so he would say. They would believe him for a long time until God revealed divine truth. I thought, "I know I'm not perfect, but I'm not doing the many things he's telling people I'm doing." I would ask them, "Do you think my husband would let me take all his money?" He told everybody I was taking his money and smoking crack when he was smoking crack like he couldn't stop. I was trying. The smoke intake was too hard for me. That's why I had to have weed with mine.

He would tell his mom that I didn't cook or wash his clothes. She always believed her son, and when I put him in jail, she didn't care for me the more. Nobody has a right to keep hitting me repeatedly for no reason. I can speak on that because I was abusive to one of my children's fathers. I would just hit him if he didn't respond a certain way or lied or cheated. (That was so uncool) I never put my hands on Tony until I just got fed up.

We want to thank sister two for coming around and speaking the truth to him. We also thank her for helping us when we were in a hard spot. She said she wouldn't help him. She was only doing it for me, but she was so flip-floppy you never know what to believe about her. She's like my husband, trying to portray an image to keep from being hurt or allowing people to see the real them with a tender heart.

We have been through some things. We thank our children for always being there, even during unbearable times. I'm proud of the respect they show and the forgiveness they have extended to both of us. The forgiveness didn't come with ease. The truth is, it's not fully there with all my children, but they know the principle of God's word regarding respect.

Have there been some words of hurt expressed? Of course, I'm their Mom, but God's foundation in their lives is healing us all, to God be the Glory.

We genuinely like to thank our parents and my Grandmother (Momma Boots, who's no longer here, I dedicate this to her for all her words of wisdom and silent prayers). We wore our parents out to the point my dad said, "I know you love this man, and I'm going to stay out of this. I have two failed marriages, and you must figure this out."

Tony's mom stated she didn't like me because of my skin color, but over the years, she's liked me (at least that's what he says, and Sister 3 says. They believe she has issues with color). I think, at times, she knows I'm good to her son. For years, her son was very rude, controlling, and bossy to her until I started telling him about respecting her regardless of how she treats me. "That's your mom." He was also angry with her because she never left his dad or put him in jail. He was full of anger for many reasons. Growing up, he dealt with not having enough food, people teasing him because of how he dressed, people close to him violating him, and sharing a room with four siblings. He also had to endure his dad whooping him almost every day, constantly ridiculing him, calling him gay, and so much more. He says he's forgiven his father but becomes angry again when you talk about certain things.

We also thank every person who truly prayed for us, especially my children, my dad, Clarence Cooper, the late Helen Cooper, my mom-grandmother, and my birth mother Linda Cooper, whom I must tell she has to respect my husband. (She still has to forgive; God is still working on her. I told him not long ago that he and mom will have the best son and mother-in-law relationship.) I also thank Apostle Charlie and the late Valarie Gates-Kimpson, Apostle Rodgers-Butler, Dr. Felicia and Apostle Cunningham, Apostle Charlene McCoy, Apostle Cooper T. Lane, Apostle Sherry Burch, and Timoyln Jetter, my spiritual mother who pushed me to move forward in God, along with Dr. Charmaine Powell, and many more.

Tony says, "I would like to thank God. I know Him for myself in my way. I want to thank my mom, whom I love dearly, my daughter, Sasha, and my stepchildren. I also want to apologize for all the pain my family caused. I love you all.

I also would like to thank Mr. Ivy and his lovely wife,

Bobby Zamore and Micheal Zamore, for praying for me the day I got shot and all of Bay City that prayed that day."

Antonio and Marsha Gonzales

TABLE OF CONTENTS

Chapter 1 – The Day We Met   *Pg. 1*

Chapter 2 - We Said, "We Do!"   *Pg. 9*

Chapter 3 - Van Vleck, Texas   *Pg. 39*

Chapter 4 - My Husband's Gunshot   *Pg. 49*

Chapter 5 - Leaving Bay City   *Pg. 61*

Chapter 6 - 'Till Death Do Us Part *Pg. 71*

Chapter 7 - Done This Time For Real *Pg. 75*

Chapter 8 - I Let Him Back   *Pg. 81*

Chapter 9 - Enough Is Enough   *Pg.103*

Antonio and Marsha Gonzales

ACKNOWLEDGMENTS

Lord, I want to say thank You for allowing Antonio and me to write this book. This book is dedicated to You, our Lord and Savior. You've given us the grace and mercy to be able to write this book—twenty-three years of a broken marriage that pushed us to find You, and I'm forever grateful. We also dedicate this book to our families, who have told us we needed to go on our separate ways. Still, our trust is in You, Lord; Your word has displayed the impossible.

Mark 10:9, "Therefore what God has joined together, let no one separate." (CSB)

Antonio and Marsha Gonzales

INTRODUCTION

Before you go deep into this book, I'm telling you that God instructed me to write as I was led. I went back and forth with Him, and He said, "Write it as I instruct you and be transparent." My husband is 100% on board, and he agrees.

Some of this book is hard to read but always remember that spirits are real; it's not the person. Sometimes this book has been hard to write because we had to deal with our past and ourselves. At times, dealing with the man or woman in the mirror is not easy, but to move forward and be healed, we have to accept our part and take full accountability - not blaming anyone, but assuming that some people can't impart the right things in life if they don't know the right thing. We are not making excuses but just accepting the truth.

John 8:32, "And ye shall know the truth, and the truth shall make you free." (KJV)

Ephesians 6:12, "For our struggle is not against enemies of blood and flesh, but against the rulers, against the authorities, against the cosmic powers of this present darkness, against the spiritual forces of evil in the heavenly places." (NRSV)

My husband and I were both believers when we met, but our relationship with Christ hadn't yet reached a personal level. I think I just got saved a year before and wasn't reading or applying the word. He came from a Catholic background but always felt it was much more to salvation than Virgin Mary and the Rosary. During this journey, we learned that Christ is the head of our lives as well as the head of our marriage. We are two broken people from different cultures, coming together as one with much baggage and soul ties, but God. We hope our story will help you understand that our Lord and Savior can do the impossible.

Matthew 19:26, "Jesus looked at them and said, "With man this is impossible, but with God all things are possible." (CSB)

CHAPTER 1

THE DAY WE MET

Marsha: It was a hot day in August 1999. I was on West Blvd. selling plates with my old church, Hedges and Highway under Bishop Exodus Rodgers. This short man came up to me and ordered a plate. He just kept staring at me, and in my mind, I thought, "What was he looking at?"

(Keep in mind I still had a lot of flesh, not too much Holy Ghost, and honestly, I was just coming into the knowledge of the trinity: The Father, The Son, and The Holy Ghost.)

This man had on a tee shirt and some light-colored Levi's. They had holes in them, and he had on a baseball cap. To me, he was just

1

another person. So, after he got his food, he asked for my number and said, "You're going to be my wife." I replied, "I don't know about that because I don't date outside my race."

No offense to Latinos, but I don't even think I knew much about a Latin person. Tony said God told him that his wife was across the street when he was inside working. So, I told him, "If God sends you across my path again, then fine, but until then, I'll see you later!"

So, about a week later, guess who comes into Taco Bell? Mr. Gonzalez! We exchanged conversations and decided to meet at my home. At that time, I was selling drugs, smoking weed, fornicating with my child's father, reading my Bible, asking for deliverance, and feeling heavy convictions. I was warring with this flesh. *Romans 13:13-14, "Because we belong to the day, we must live decent lives for all to see. Don't participate in the darkness of wild parties and drunkenness, or sexual promiscuity and immoral living, or in quarreling and jealousy. Instead, clothe yourself with the presence of the Lord Jesus. And don't let yourself think about ways to indulge your evil desires." (NLT)*

Even though I wasn't reading the word as I should have, I remembered things preachers talked about that would send me to hell. I never forgot that thing; having sex and not being married was one.

Tony and I would hang out, talk, and entertain each other, but the conviction was harrowing. We would be intimate, a conviction would come, and I would have to stop. Tony would ask, "What's wrong?"

"I can't keep going against God. I can't do this!"

We stopped having sex and chilled out for a while. Tony would come by, smoke a blunt and chill, then go home. When I'd get home from work, he would have cut my grass and bushes and spent time with my dog. Tony would ask me to marry him, and I would say no. He asked three times. So, we chilled for a minute. When we were apart, my son, Dante, came to me. He was seven years old and asked, "Mom, can I talk to you like a big boy?" I replied, "Yes!"

Now, please remember that Dante didn't know anything about Tony wanting to marry me.

Dante said, "Mom, this man will be in your life forever. Promise me he won't take my place!"

I said, "How do you know?"

He just said, "I know!"

Tony and I told our families, and I don't know everyone's actual response, but we were married four months later. My sister-in-law, number one, tried to warn me about her brother. She never knew who we were as individuals, let alone as a couple, and that we were coming together as one.

Matthew 19:5-6, "For this reason, a man will leave his father and mother and be joined to his wife, and the two will become one flesh. So, they are no longer two, but one flesh. Therefore, what God joined together, let no one separate." (NIV)

Antonio:

My wife was beautiful, and I loved the Jesus in her. My wife was always happy. I loved that.

Marsha:

My husband was starting to look so sexy to me. I loved when he would come by my house all dirty after working hard and still tend to my needs. I needed him to ensure I was okay, cut the grass, trim my hedges, and tend to my dog. He also tended to my weed habit at the time. I loved his work ethic and him always trying to do for me; it was just that sense of security. Again, we were not sharing the bad things from our past. We were happy to have found comfort within each other then. We had not talked about our future much, but we talked about having children. Again, we enjoyed each other's company. We just kept saying we loved each other.

Before we got married, I remember it had snowed. My husband was so excited. That's when I learned we were two different people. He had never seen snow before, and there it was. I come from the Midwest, where all we got every winter was snow, so that was my first abnormal awakening. I want to say there was so much cultural awakening from our different backgrounds and upbringing. We were so different on many levels, but we couldn't deal with much in the beginning. You will see how we opened up on many different levels as you read.

Revelation 22:13, "I am the Alpha and the Omega, the first and the Last, the beginning and the end." (NIV)

Psalm 15:3, "The Lord is watching everywhere, keeping his eye on both the evil and the good." (NLT)

CHAPTER 2

WE SAID, "WE DO!"

Marsha: Tony and I married in June of 2000. My son, my dad, stepmom at the time, stepsister, grandmother, and Angie came without hesitation. We married at the courthouse, and after we were married, I remember my dad warning, "Two strong-headed people... how is this going to work?" I didn't realize that my dad was seeing what I couldn't see back then. I pondered on that statement for years and now understand that being a submissive wife was not an option for me at the beginning of this marriage. Honestly, I didn't know about the Virtuous Woman at this point in my walk with God.

Proverbs 31:10-31, "Who can find a virtuous wife? For her worth is far above rubies.

The heart of her husband safely trusts her; So he will have no lack of gain. She does him good and not evil All the days of her life. She seeks wool and flax And willingly works with her hands. She is like the merchant ships. She brings her food from afar. She also rises while it is yet night. And provides food for her household, And a portion for her maidservants. She considers a field and buys it; From her profits she plans a vineyard. She girds her strength And strengthens her arm. She perceives that her merchandise is good, And her lamp does not go out by night. She stretches out her hands to the distaff, And her hand holds the spindle. She extends her hand to the poor, yes, she reaches out her hands to the needy. She is not afraid of snow for her household, For all her household is clothed with scarlet. She makes tapestry for herself; Her clothing is fine linen and purple. Her husband is known in the gates, When he sits among the elders of the land. She makes the linen garments and sells them, And supplies sashes for the merchants. Strength and honor are her clothing. She shall rejoice in time to come. She opens her mouth with wisdom, And on her tongue is the law of kindness. She watches over the ways of her household, And does not eat the bread of idleness. Her children rise up and call her blessed; Her husband also and he praises her; Many daughters have done well, but you excel them all. Charm is deceitful, and beauty is passing. But a woman who fears the Lord, she shall be praised. Give her of the fruit of her hands, And let her own works praise her in the gates." (NKJV)

Ephesians 5:22-25, "Wives, submit to your own husbands, as to the Lord. For their husband is the head of the wife, as also Christ is head of the church; and he is the savior of the body. Therefore, just as the church is subject to Christ, so let the wives be to their own husbands in everything. Husbands, love your wives, just as Christ also loved the church and gave Himself for her." (NKJV)

Tony and I didn't understand all that, and we didn't have counsel until after the fact, which caused mistake number one. We knew we couldn't keep sleeping together without marriage, but he was cool about us not having sex. We just had a friendship that was so peaceful. We could talk and laugh without any fussing. He prayed with me, discussed his childhood experiences with God, and knew the Word. *(At least that's what I thought until I said, "I do!")*

At the beginning of our marriage, I didn't see the drug addiction, his hot temperament, the flirtation, the control, the bossiness, his 'my way or no way attitude,' the dominating mentality, his being a ladies' man, a jealous and aggressive man, and one with so many more spirits. All I saw was a kind-hearted, caring, hardworking, compassionate, church-talking, always smiling, making me laugh, and helping with my needs, man.

I wasn't overjoyed to be getting married, but I was thankful. My husband says he was more excited than I was because he said he was so in love. I was happy, but after all the brokenness I had endured, I was thankful because it wasn't that fairy tale marriage. I had already had children *(I never complained about my children because they saved my life. At one point in life, they were the only reason that kept me living. I love them unconditionally.)* Yet, again, I was thankful for Antonio.

Antonio:

My wife was very kind-hearted to anybody. She was always helping others and giving her last. She was always good to her children, but her weed habit was an everyday thing. She stayed hours in the bathtub praying, and I would wait. She would smoke and talk to

God as if He were sitting face-to-face with her. I didn't understand that part, but I knew she knew God. She was so different that I would call her a "white girl" trapped in a black person's body. She loved to read and watch church programs on TV. She loves everything clean and in order. She read so many books and was always helping people, just anybody.

She and I would shock each other by bringing home strangers. She would bring strangers to our home. They would steal from her, but she remembered when no one helped her with her children, so she would never do people like that.

My dad would help, and my grandma, but my mouth had become outspoken. I didn't like people telling me stuff, and I carried unforgiveness with my dad, mom, and grandma. My dad would help, but he was sneaking to help me, causing problems for his household, so I stopped asking.

I started growing in maturity, and God taught me that I couldn't help everyone. I asked my wife to promise she would never change for anyone, not even me.

Marsha:

At that point in our marriage, Tony only saw the surface of me, not the healing process needed to move forward. I was still so broken; I had childhood scars, emotional baggage, unresolved self-issues, and soul ties with their baggage.

Come to think of it, Tony and I both had baggage. I was carrying the spirits of rejection, anger, insecurity, hatred, bitterness, disappointment from self and others, poor self-esteem, sense of failure, denial, lying, loneliness, overprotective, distrust, and betrayal. I had no feelings toward other people except my children. I was distant, withdrawn, serious, short-tempered, fighting spirits, rage, and a few more. Yet we still moved forward and said, "I do." I was masking so much hurt but still trying to stand as a Christian. I didn't know I was a bleeding saint at that time. I didn't understand the notion of becoming of one flesh. I always prayed to know what it meant to become one flesh, and as we grew together over the years, I've learned a lot.

Let's talk about the "I do" part.

After we walked down the courthouse steps, Tony said, "You're mine now!" The tone he used gave me chills. I thought, "What the what?" I brushed it off, but I never forgot it. As days passed, something one of Tony's friends said came back to me. She said, "Why would you be with a guy like this? You seem too nice for him!" In my mind, I thought, "What kind of guy is this?" Wow, okay! Let's take this journey. It was my first rude awakening to the godly man I married.

One day, I found Tony outside on the deck.

It was cold; he was standing there and had been there for hours. I asked him if he was okay or what was wrong with him. He replied, "I'm fine. I have to tell you something!" I thought, "What?" He said, "I do a little coke!" Being a little delayed in my choices of drugs back then, I wondered, "What's that?" I thought, "What the ****?"

I noticed Tony struggled to smoke weed. He didn't like to be one that puff, puff, pass, and give. He would say, "I'm good!" My choice was weed, and his was coke. We were two broken people abusing drugs to deal with life. It wasn't social drug use either; it was an everyday lifestyle for him and me, mainly weekends at first.

One night, I woke up with Tony standing over me with a knife. I started praying and talking to him. He was speechless, and I remember him going to the kitchen. I started rebuking the spirits of rage, murder, and others and pleading with the blood of Jesus. His body began moving funny, and his whole countenance changed in my face. He went from a confused dude to Tony (Pretty boy, as I used to call him. Tony always kept a fresh haircut with a baseball cap turned around backward). That's when I tapped into my first lesson about demons and imps. Crazy, right? But real.

My first deliverance experience was in my kitchen on Central Avenue with my husband. He kept asking, "What happened to me? Why do I feel funny?" I never told him until years later. I hear you all saying, "Girl, naw! This marriage is over! This dude is crazy! Not me! You are crazy, and your kids are there? Nope, it's over!"

Yeah, that's what I thought, too. I was wrestling back and forth, questioning God every time. I was becoming like Gideon, who wanted a sign from God.

Judges 6:36-40, "And Gideon said unto

God, If thou wilt save Israel by mine hand, as thou hast said, Behold, I will put a fleece of wool in the floor; and if the dew be on the fleece only, and it be dry upon all the earth beside, then shall I know that thou wilt save Israel by mine hand, as thou hast said. And it was so: for he rose up early on the morrow, and thrust the fleece together, and wringed the dew out of the fleece, a bowl full of water. And Gideon said unto God, Let not thine anger be hot against me, and I will speak but this once: let me prove, I pray thee, but this once with the fleece; let it now be dry only upon the fleece, and upon all the ground let there be dew. And God did so that night: for it was dry upon the fleece only, and there was dew on all the ground." (KJV)

After 23 years, I felt that I followed everything I believed was God. Again, the man said no, but I took my marriage vows seriously. My father was even disappointed in my choice. My father felt as though my husband was selfish.

Tony was so proud of how he looked on our wedding day, and my dad thought he should be more concerned with how I looked. At that time, I understood my husband's liking for material things. He came from hard struggle, and there I was. Everything was given to me, and when I moved to Charlotte, that was the first thing God dealt with me about. That's why I loved Tony even more.

One night we had a big argument (an exchange of diverging or opposite views, typically a heated or angry one) over me throwing away leftover food. To me, it was just food. I didn't know that my husband had it hard with food from time to time growing up. At a very young age, he would have to work hard and not receive his hard labor, and sometimes he would work just for food.

I was materialistic (excessively concerned with material possessions, money-oriented) and didn't value things. My mindset was that my daddy got me because my dad never said no. He was doing that to make up for my mom not being there. At least, as I looked back over my life, he was doing the best he knew how, and he always said yes.

My father told me no for the first time when I was 27. It devastated me, but he said he had to do it so I could grow up. In all that processing, God taught me how to be thankful and appreciate the little things.

My husband was always thankful for stuff in the beginning. Again, our backgrounds were colliding (hit with force when moving). I always wanted to buy things with a name brand when he could wear something to keep him covered. *(Don't get it twisted. He could dress, but by then, I was finding out that he was some drug dealer, tattoo artist, and a lady's man who loved coke.)* From his point of view, "I've married a daddy's girl, spoiled rotten, high class, educated, a church-going girl with four children who are always cleaning up. Can I handle this? I'm just trying to live to see 25!"

Well, things were about to get a little rough. Just remember, spirits are real, and I was moving by the Spirit of God. I asked the Lord several things: to have an anointing like Him, love people unconditionally like Him, and see my husband inside out. What did I do that for?

1 John 5:14-15, "We are confident that he hears us whenever we ask for anything pleases him. And since we know he hears us when we make our requests, we also know that he will give us what we ask for." (NLT)

And no, staying in an abusive situation is not okay. This is how I believe the Holy Ghost took me. His divine covering was always there with me because everything leads to Him, not my flesh, not a woman who couldn't be without a man or some good sex; it was none of that. It was just my assessment. Tony was my husband, best friend, counselor, business partner, and future son's father.

Now, Lord, as my readers begin this journey, walk with them. I plead the blood of Jesus over their minds and thinking process. I ask that the words on these pages bring clarity, healing, deliverance, understanding, revelation, guidance, and truth to those in similar circumstances. I pray you will allow God to strengthen you to trust the process and lean not to your own understanding. God gets all the glory and God only.

Isaiah 42:8-9, "I am the Lord; that is my name! I will not give my glory to anyone else, nor share my praise with carved idols. Everything I prophesied has come true, and now I will prophesy again. I will tell you the future before it happens." (NLT)

Even in the short time of being married, I noticed my husband would act differently when we were out in public. He always worried about what people thought of our relationship. He would start acting funny as if he was ashamed of me being black. He states it wasn't that, but I always felt like people's approval of him was important. Yes, it was rejection (the dismissing or refusing of a proposal, idea, etc.). Growing up, being rejected by people who are supposed to love you the most brings about a longing for acceptance. We both had that spirit upon us, causing us so much pain when both our parents were not accepting of what we loved so much in each other. Even though my dad was never rude to Tony, my mother, Linda, told him at times that she didn't care for him, which hurt him and me. His mom and others in his family made it known, but my love for Christ and him always gave me a "forty times forty" forgiving spirit.

Matthew 18:21-22, "Then Peter came to

him and asked," Lord, how often should I forgive someone who sins against me? Seven times." no, not seven times," Jesus replied, "but seventy times seventy." (NLT)

When Tony acted funny, I would start questioning God. "Did I miss You? Did I move in my flesh?" I prayed repeatedly, fasted, and reached out to the counselor. Yet and still, God would give me that peace.

Even though Tony and I would hear others say how attractive we were, we struggled with poor self-esteem. So again, the attention Tony longed for was a cover-up from some buried secrets he and I had carried all our lives which affected our sexual relationship as a married couple. We both had been molested, which affected us severely. We also experienced multiple soul ties from past relationships and casual sex partners. *(There's not a day that I don't thank God for sparing me from contracting*

HIV/AIDS. Glory!) We were a hot mess. A touch from him would make me shut down, push him away, and open the door for the devil, which took him back to a place of rejection. It sent me back into all the hands that should not have touched me.

1 Corinthians 7:3-5, "The husband should fulfill his wife's sexual needs, and the wife should fulfill her husband's needs. The wife gives authority over her body to her husband, and the husband gives authority over his body to his wife. Do not deprive each other of sexual relations, unless you both agree to refrain from sexual intimacy for a limited time so you can give yourselves more completely to prayer. Afterward, you should come together again so that Satan won't be able to tempt you because of your lack of self-control." (NLT)

My husband's touch brought back unhealed issues. What was worse was that his need for approval hurt him because I was dealing with my struggles, too. I was a train wreck. Let me keep it one hundred. We didn't notice the problem was there on my side until I started going to counseling and stopped using drugs. Drugs were a numbing medication; they took away all the bad memories and failures. (At least, that's what I told myself) The drugs increased libido (sex drive or desire for sex), yet I was accustomed to using drugs just to be intimate. I could never have sex with anyone while I was sober except my husband. Granted, I have four children, but none yet from my husband.

My husband's and my bond is undeniable (unable to be denied or disputed). I never knew what true intimacy was until I met my husband. Down through the years, we are still growing in intimacy. (An intimate relationship is an interpersonal relationship that involves physical or emotional intimacy. There are four types of intimacy: emotional, mental, spiritual, and physical.) After all these years, we are learning the levels of intimacy shared by Dr. Barbara Wilson of Family Life Canada.

They are "1. safe communication 2. our opinions, beliefs, and cultures 3. personal opinions and beliefs 4. our feelings and experiences 5. our needs, emotions, and desires."

Through all the wrestling, did I make the right decision? God would keep telling me I was in control no matter what I thought.

My husband said he wanted a change, and we struggled a little bit. We both had poor financial management and didn't value a dollar. We were wasteful spenders, and two broken people were coming together as one. We were still learning from one another and hiding from each other. I used to say my husband completed me, and God said, "Not so!"

At one point, Tony met my brother, who is now deceased. I remember him saying, "You sure you want him around me?" I was like, "I trust him!"

My, my, my. My life in Saint Louis was never the same. I was the last to know; everybody knew but me. I was always at home reading my Bible, working, and staying out of the way. Tony, on the other hand, was doing everything under the sun. He was cheating, selling drugs, staying out overnight, abusing drugs, and so much more.

I will never forget the first time that dude (Tony) hit me. I was driving down the street in Holland and saw Corey Rusan. I asked him, "Why does God keep waking me to pray for you at night?" He raised his shirt and had something under his shirt. He told me he was having kidney issues. We talked, I introduced him to Tony, and then we drove off. The next thing I knew was that dude stole me in my face. It caught me off guard, and I just cried and said, "What's wrong with you?" He responded that I disrespected him. I thought, "God, what in the world is this? You don't bless with sorrow!" My mind started wandering, "This dude ain't from God! There is no way this ****** just hit me for no reason!"

I was going to my daddy's house, so I had to pull myself together and act like everything was peaches and cream. At that point, the spirit of fear had taken root (an unpleasant emotion caused by the belief that someone or something is dangerous, likely to cause pain or a threat). I was just confused at that point. I thought, "Why would that dude hit me? Was it because I talked to my lifelong childhood friend?" I had to consider our cultural differences and six other spirits operating between us: insecurity, control, dominance, aggression, rage, and abuse. All of those spirits stemmed from the main root of rejection.

Tony never apologized for his actions or said anything about the matter. He wasn't sorry, but he was out of control. He maintained a calm exterior in front of my family, but behind closed doors, he tried to intimidate me (frighten or overawe someone, especially to make them do what one wants). During that time, my children were afraid, too. We all were, and I didn't know who to talk to but God. I was just as scared to call the cops.

The six months we spent in St. Louis were a mess. Everyone was seeing my husband out at clubs and just about everywhere, but I wasn't seeing him. He wasn't answering my calls or responding to me, but I prayed and fasted for thirty days to keep him safe. I was so worried and prayed so much for him that I looked like a drug addict, even though I wasn't using at the time. I was just a praying wife who interceded nonstop for my husband.

From time to time, Tony would come by the house and get drugs from the ceiling. Once he left, it would be days before I saw him again. He would bring me some money or have one of the guys come to check on me, and then he would keep it moving. People would tell me they saw Tony in the mall with another woman. I was so broken that I thought, "I am hurt, destroyed, and shattered!" I became ill and eventually passed out at work. My dad came to take me home. The stress was taking a toll on me. On the other hand, Tony was somewhere getting high, cheating, or just partying. To this day, he says it was never about the women; he just loved his drugs.

I will never forget the last night Tony left our apartment on the south side. God told me he was sending him into the wilderness. That dude was making crazy money and leaving me in the house alone with the weed bags. So, I would go in them, use what I wanted, and call people over to use with me. "Come smoke and chill," I told them. I was simultaneously smoking, praying, and calling on the name of Jesus. Tony found out and pulled knives on my child and me. At that point, I was scared to death of him.

One day, I went around my now-deceased brother with a black eye. He made me stay at his shop while he talked with Tony. When he returned, he warned me. "I am going to handle this, but if you are going to be with him, I will leave it alone." Little did he know that I was still holding on to what God said, even though my circumstances were contrary to the character of Christ. Tony was getting into all kinds of trouble, and he had to stay away from me because he was too much. I will never forget what my eyes saw; I thought I was dreaming.

At that point, I knew my dude was a Mexican *vato*, like in those movies. The drug activities were beyond me. I was a simple church woman trying to be a wife and do right by God and my children. Tony, on the other hand, was sinking deeper and deeper into trouble.

Eventually, I called his parole officer and told them he needed to be paroled to Texas. They heeded my warning and had him paroled the next day. They gave him five days to get home, and then he was gone. I was deeply saddened but relieved in the same breath.

I hated living in St. Louis, and Tony made me look stupid in my hometown. The women I thought was cool was trying to get with him. I should have let them get with him because he was only flirting because of his insecurities (uncertainty or anxiety about oneself; lack of confidence).

Exodus 20:17, "Thou shalt not covet thy neighbour's house, thou shalt not covet thy neighbour's wife, nor his manservant, nor his maidservant, nor his ox, nor his ass, nor any thing that is thy neighbour's." (KJV)

Eventually, I filed for divorce and returned to Charlotte. Little did I know an angelic visitation would occur two days in a row. In my first experience, I was sleeping on the couch. A bright light hovered over my coffee table and grew brighter in intensity. I heard the angelic voice say, "Go to Texas with your husband."

I was overwhelmed by this presence, and I couldn't move. Nevertheless, I responded. Then it said, "Sell everything in your home and go!" The bright presence left after that message. I just sat there looking around the apartment, unable to move. I was immobilized for about thirty minutes, and all I remember saying was, "Glory, glory, glory!"

The following day, I woke up still thinking about what happened. While trying to figure out what was what, I grabbed my phone to call a friend I always talked to about the Bible. For some reason, my phone wouldn't dial out, so I went to the neighbor's and used her phone to call my number to see if it would work. I heard a recording stating my service was interrupted. Somehow, I ended up calling Tony, and we had a conversation. He told me he messed up and wanted to go to counseling. I declined and said, "Nope, I'm good! I need time to myself!" Bear in mind that my phone wouldn't work; however, when I called Tony, it worked. Curious now, I hung up with Tony and tried to call my dad, but the call dropped. I said, "Okay, God! Really!" Then Tony called, and my phone worked!! I was so amused! "God, what is it?" I ran back to the neighbor's and tried my phone, but there was nothing. Then I called Tony, and the phone worked. "God, I know it's You! You want me to go to Texas!"

My dad was upset about my decision, but as usual, he commented, "You're grown! You are going to do what you want to do!"

I had a moving sale, packed up, and

prepared my daughter and me to leave town. Before I left, I drove by my cousin Latonya's house. I parked my car, got out, walked up the street, and started praying. Suddenly, I felt a powerful impact in my left eye. The pain was indescribable; all I remember saying was, "Lord, whoever is ever going to have this type of accident, don't let it kill them!" (Ponder on this for a few chapters) Bear in mind that I was walking and praying when this happened. The pain only lasted a few brief seconds, but it was excruciating.

I just stood still in my tracks, asking God what that was. "What are you trying to tell me?" I asked, but there was no answer. Nevertheless, I returned to my car, drove to the Bell, said my goodbyes, and my daughters and I hit the road, headed to Van Vleck, Texas. I trusted God and the encounter I had just a few nights ago.

Antonio and Marsha Gonzales

CHAPTER 3

VAN VLECK, TEXAS

As I drove, I asked God, "Are You sure this is You because I was already getting ready to move back to Charlotte and file for divorce?"

In that short eight months, I found out Mr. Gonzalez was a verbally and physically abusive man. I already wanted to leave, but the pull for me to go was so strong, and I was so in love at that time. I believed God to heal my marriage despite how angry I was.

I made it to Texas without realizing I was on assignment (a task or piece of work assigned to someone as part of a job or course of study). There was a lot I had endured in St. Louis that I still grappled with.

Back in the day, my husband became a connection in St. Louis, which was when his behavior toward me started changing. He was arrogant and thought he was every woman's gift. No, it wasn't that! He was just something new and unfamiliar (not known or recognized), and he especially loved women's attention. Now, Tony was a man who went from having nothing to everything and felt as if *all eyes were on him*. He was a man oppressed with a heavy rejection spirit. He said, "Now I'm getting all attention, and they need me to make it happen!"

We were supposed to be one; then he would start saying that I was jealous of him (feeling or showing envy of someone for their achievements and advantages). I looked at him, thinking, "You are stupid! Nothing you are doing is Godly! The devil is just setting you up! None of this money or material things you've gained is from God; the devil is setting you up!"

Then I thought, "Wow, God! Why would you send me here?" As I entered the town, my car broke down. It wouldn't work. I wasn't in town for two days when Tony left my girls and me at his mom's house (she doesn't care for me, and her actions made it known). I discovered he returned to Saint Louis while I was with his mom, where I was unwanted. So, I found a shelter in Bay City for my daughters and me.

I was already stuck. My car was not working, and the mechanic said I needed a new engine, so I looked stupid. I learned Tony brought women to his mom's house while we were married. He was running back and forth like nothing, and I was praying and fasting for him, looking like a crackhead. I did not know anyone while facing those challenges in Bay City until I met the Nellews. They were pastors who took my children and me in. They had property, a vacant house that they opened up for my children and me. The Nellews provided everything we needed.

I had a place to stay, and though Tony and I were separated, he still came around. By then, I was suppressing my crack use. I was functional, but I was so broken. That dude was dragging me, and what's worse, all my childhood baggage and life baggage was beating me down. It didn't help when my dad wouldn't let me come home. And the only person that would be sickly, and that was okay, dokie. Dad never turned me away unless my grandmother made him. He didn't want to this time, but he did so just to keep things peaceful. *(I never got mad at him. I just knew I had to find my own way.)*

God spoke to me so clearly one day. When I was getting high, the Holy Spirit said, "You love him more than you love yourself, and you don't love yourself because you don't love Me!"

I looked around the room, and He spoke again, clear as day, and a light bulb went off. Then He said, "In the midst of your mess, I got you, and this will be a teaching tool for you." During that time, I was still going through in my marriage. Tony was still being super rude. He was snorting coke and smoking crack. Me, well I was smoking Julie blunts (*weed and crushed crack*). He and I were two broken, toxic people declaring we loved each other while yet destroying one another. I was too damaged to let go, but I kept hearing God say, "I got you! I got you covered."

This might sound super crazy, but I always felt a shield around me when Tony tried to hurt me, but God kept His word. When Tony thought he was hurting me, God was protecting me. That was what I experienced. Now, please don't think I'm justifying abuse. I am talking about my own journey with God. I would never advise anyone to remain in a violent situation.

If you're in a domestic violence situation, call 1-800-799-7233, and they will help you.

So, things became barren, and God was the only person I could lean on. Our conversations were very intense, and I was just seeking Him to make Himself known to me. I was fussing because I was saying, "Why would you have me go through this, and all these pastors are saying, "God wouldn't do that to you?" Then He reminded me, saying, "Remember when you said you wanted to see your husband inside out and know why he acted the way He did? And do you remember when you asked for an anointing like mine to love people unconditionally with my real love? Why are you being moved by what I'm allowing? I chose you; nothing is surprising. Why do you keep running to people who are in the same situation as you but try to lie to you? Trust Me; learn My voice for yourself and know that I am God."

Back then, I was so thirsty for answers and deliverance that I was running to talk to anybody. The devil blinded me because people were human, just like me. Some were just preaching the word and not living anything, barely making it themselves.

As time progressed, again, I found myself at Tony's mom's house, talking about a dream I had. I dreamed I was cleaning his bottom at the hospital, and the nurses were making faces because he stunk so badly. We joked about it, but we never ever knew it was a warning - a prophetic dream (accurately describing or predicting what will happen in the future). I dealt with it briefly, but I pondered on it more, and of course, Mr. Gonzalez was still moving the way he moved. He didn't react to the warning, at least not to me, because he hated it when I would tell him things.

I was miserable, wretchedly unhappy, uncomfortable, depressed, and at the lowest point ever. I felt like a failure as a mom and non-productive in everything. I was tormented by so many emotions that ran through my mind. I had more than the pain I experienced from my marriage; I had pain from the various places of rejection I experienced in my childhood. Rejection was a critical factor that brought forth so many attachments (an extra part or extension that can be attached to something to perform a particular function. For example, anger, anxiety, depression, sadness, rage, hurt, jealousy, withdrawal, suicide, and many more).

The night before Mr. Gonzalez was shot, he asked if he could go out with his friends. I looked at him like he was crazy because he never questioned whether I minded if he went anywhere. I said, "I think you should stay home, but it's up to you!" Needless to say, he told his friends he was going to chill. He didn't go anywhere, but they wanted to use our car. I was like, "No! What for? They have their own cars!"

Tony went into the room and watched T.V. That night, a few of his buddies got into a minor altercation (a noisy argument or disagreement, especially in public), but thankfully Tony wasn't there. He had nothing to do with it, and I was grateful to God. I told him, "See, you didn't go for a reason!" We didn't know that only 22 hours later, he would be shot in the face.

As we write, Mr. Gonzalez is still warring with himself and the personal issues that hinder him from submitting to God. In his case, medical doctors told me one thing, but my God said He knew better. "When Tony obeys me, I will release his hand and restore all that was lost, for he is wrestling with the flesh and spirit."

As I reflect, I know God is genuinely breaking me even the more. I'm not where I want to be but thank God I'm not the same Marsha Cooper I used to be. I was a broken young lady with many issues. I was unstable and viewed everything through the lenses of a child (the characteristic attitude of mind or way of thinking of a person or group.) Life's journey will take you places and require you to shift to adapt to your surroundings just to survive, but one touch from God will refocus and realign you (change or restore to a different or former position or state.) God will also give you wisdom and knowledge that you can't imagine. When I said yes to God, things became more apparent. Something my dad used to say when I was a kid made sense to me then, and the blinders were removed.

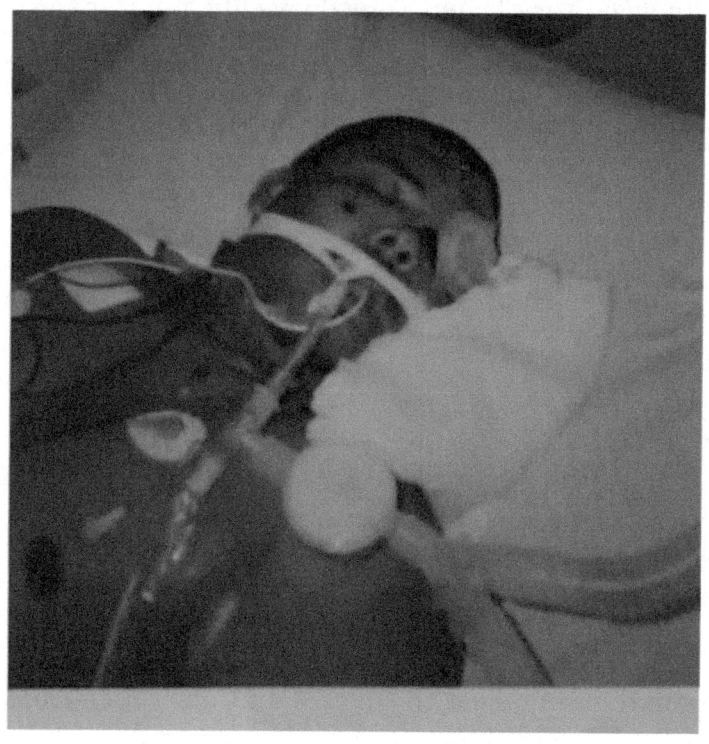

CHAPTER 4

MY HUSBAND'S GUNSHOT

I'll never forget that November day. It was around 11:20 am when my sister-in-law knocked on my door. Tears rolled down her face as she informed me that Tony had been shot.

About a month before Tony was shot, God started talking to me a lot. I was all alone, far from anything I had ever known, so God became my best friend. My family wasn't that important to me because all I had to depend on was my dad and grandma. My uncle was in prison, and my brother was dealing with his own demons. Needless to say, my circle became really small when I turned 19 and left home. My children were all I had besides Tony. The Lord and I would meet in Van Vleck, Texas, under a big tree in the cemetery. That was my quiet place where my daughters and I would stay for hours and just talk to God and each other. At that point, my children were affected by our poor decisions in many ways. They were separated from their families, and everything familiar was taken away. Worse, they were being mistreated by people I thought I could trust. The most shameful part was that I was so broken that I wasn't connecting to them as their mother. Once, they told me that when I married Tony, everything changed. They said that the things we used to do and places we would go, we just didn't go. Little did they know that I was fighting for my life. I was trying not to give up, kill myself, or give them up to their families. Never mind that I was fighting drug addiction and battling mental and physical abuse, I was going through a dry and rough patch in my life.

Bear in mind that with everything else I was facing at the time, I still had demons from my past to deal with. I was still suffering from rejection in my childhood. I kept asking why she didn't want me. I struggled with that until my late 40s, over ten years ago. Thank God that I'm healed.

It was 11:20 pm when my sister law came knocking on the door. I knew it was about Tony because something hit my stomach when he got shot. I knew deep within that something was wrong with Tony. I started praying and pacing my floor for two hours before anybody reached out because I already knew my husband was down. Regardless of anything, we could always feel each other if something was wrong with the other. No matter how mean he was to me, he would never let anyone mistreat me; we were just that toxic.

I was prepared for that gunshot incident when I felt the impact on my eye about three months before it happened. Even in my mess of smoking crack, I always talked to God and read my Bible. I believe that kept me from losing myself to the addiction that destroyed many others' lives. Many crack addicts are looked down on and judged for what the drug has done to them. I could smoke ten rocks with my weed over several days at a time. On the other hand, my husband felt as if I was going to bust my chest open, but once he started using, he would keep going. He would start with $600, but by the time he was done, he would be left with $100.

Proverbs 4:13, "Hold on to instructions, do not let it go; guard it well, for it is your life." (NIV)

God gave me divine instructions for how to pray for Tony. He would tell me to anoint his shoes, toothbrush, underpants, and car daily. I questioned, "God, why?" But He never answered me. He just said to do it, so when Tony's sister began to speak to me, God was also speaking to me. I heard Him as clear as day. God allowed Tony to be shot because of his disobedience. "I warned him to stop hanging out, and he refused to listen." The peace of God dropped instantly on me (I had never felt that level of peace before. That was the first time, and I prayed with instructions and wanted to be the last).

Psalms 115:3, "Our God, is in the heavens; he does all that he pleases." (ESV)

God does as He chooses. See the following: Genesis 39:1-23; 2 Corinthians 12:7; Daniel 4:35; and Isaiah 46:10.

I had to get ready and drive one hour and about fifteen minutes to Houston. When I arrived at the hospital, Tony was already in surgery. The bullet pierced through his left eye and shifted his brain downward. They had to remove a fourth of his brain in the front lobe. He still has bullet fragments that couldn't be removed (unsafe for him). Tony also has a metal plate holding up his brain in the front.

On that first night of surgery, the doctor informed me that he would be a vegetable if he made it through the night. He said I should not get my hopes up. Once he told me that, I called every prayer line I knew, and prayers went up. It was a tough time because Tony was cheating. Some lady told me she was pregnant, and his siblings were not getting along at all. They didn't want me to allow certain siblings to come to the hospital. It was just a crazy time. Then, his mother was being mean to me and blaming me for what had happened. I was so hurt, but I was listening to God. One day his doctor made it clear to the family, "Whatever his wife said, that's it!"

I was being lied to about everything. Tony had a friend named Angel, who warned, "Don't you leave him!" He encouraged me to stand beside Tony and the pastor from Rose of Sharon.

I was the only black person there, filling the waiting room. I could only imagine the conversations about me daily, but I was Tony's wife, trusting, praying, and believing God for it all. I had to clean, care for him, and watch him learn to walk, talk, speak, and use his hands again. To know he had been cheating while I was trying to be a good wife was quite the challenge.

"My God, why me, the little black girl from Missouri?"

My Dad also called and reminded me of what I told him. His exact words were, "You said that God told you to marry him, so why would you leave now because of people?"

I was so angry but also quite pleased when he got shot. He was mean to me and was always jealous of my children's relationship with me. He always took his frustrations out on me, primarily when he couldn't provide for me and I needed to depend on my dad. He hated that.

Before Tony started recovery, he was on a ventilator, breathing for him 100 percent. I was told he had no brain activity, but doctors couldn't understand the machine going crazy and his levels going crazy whenever people would enter his room. The nurses would have to report to his room and turn off the alarms, but everything remained calm and stable when I visited his room.

The doctors said Tony showed no brain activity and advised me to disconnect him from life support. I always kept Yolanda Adams' gospel music playing in his room. I told the doctor I needed three days to pray and fast before rendering a decision.

I drove back to Van Vleck. At that point, I was hurt but also relieved. I didn't have anybody cussing, fussing, and hitting on me. But on the other hand, I felt like, "Dag, what am I going to do? I'm responsible for this dude! I said better or worse in sickness and health."

Under the tree, I went. God and I were communicating, and He told me to tell the doctors not to remove Tony from life support.

I didn't travel to Houston on the third day. I was exhausted mentally, so I said no. Meanwhile, with no brain activity, Tony started breathing on his own, pulling on stuff, and wanting the person with the ring. Nobody knew who put the ring on him but God and me. It wasn't his wedding band. He and I had already thrown two wedding bands away (At that point in my life, I didn't realize how seriously the ring symbolized a three-strand covenant).

The nurses called to say Tony was taken off the ventilator and transferred to the unit at Herman Memorial. When I arrived, he knew me right away. Bear in mind that he didn't respond to some people quickly. I thought that was unusual, but the doctor said those kinds of patients remember the closest person and the ones they last interacted with the most. I used to ask Tony who I was. He would point to the ring and always want to hug me. The brain is amazing. I knew Tony would be okay because he wanted to kiss and hug me, trying to smile. Everyone was so amazed at how fast he was recovering.

Tony was potent all around, but it was too much for me when we returned home. He wanted to stay home with me, but his mom wanted him home with her. At that point, I was so tired. When he returned home, people picked him up as if he wasn't just shot in his head. Though he couldn't talk, he always gave the thumbs up, but nobody knew the man behind the tattoos and the stocky frame. Yes, they grew up with him, but they didn't realize the pain their friendship had caused him. He would share things that happened in his life, even as an adult, that were hard for me. Even a few siblings have stated that he was his mom's favorite, but God revealed to me his mom knows all her children, and he's just different. God chooses him through all the mistakes, disrespect, and bad decisions.

Jeremiah 1:5, "I chose you before I gave you life, and before you were born I selected you to be a prophet to the nations." (GNT)

Sleeping with the Devil

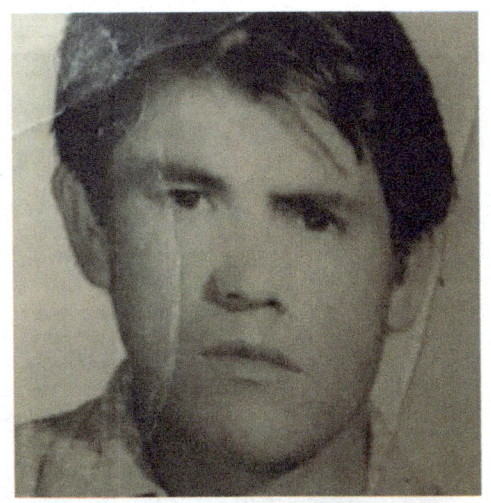

Antonio and Marsha Gonzales

CHAPTER 5

LEAVING BAY CITY

If you recall my mentioning of Bay City, you will remember that I started experiencing mechanical problems with my car. It stopped on me, and I found out I needed an engine.

Tony was released from the hospital, and God told me to lay hands on my car. (Remember, it was still at that shop where it had been for months.) I asked the technician if I could try to start my car. When I did, it cranked without any issues, while before, it wouldn't. The techs at the garage had astonished looks on their faces and asked, "What did you do?" All I could say was, "Jesus!"

I knew my assignment was up. Tony was getting better but becoming frustrated at the same time. I couldn't work and care for him, so I got myself together. I bought a car and was preparing to leave. I was so tired of Bay City and Van Vleck because I couldn't adjust. I felt like I had hit rock bottom. Tony had to learn how to walk, talk, and function again. And the attacks against me increased because I was being blamed for him being shot. What people were saying about me was unreal. Besides that, my children were being mistreated and violated. The people had crossed the line and never should have bothered them. One of them apologized, though, and I was thankful for that. The other one didn't; I still feel some way about that. Yes, I speak, but I am feeling some way. I still want to confront the person, but God said, "Not now." In their defense, my girls weren't fast or looking for attention (something I didn't learn in 2020). Bruised feelings are real and learned behavior is real. My mind still questions some of those things to this day.

Tony and I were struggling. His family mistreated my girls, but I left it all in God's hands. One of my daughters confronted the person involved in the situation, and she forgave them. She learned that forgiveness is critical and learned behavior is real.

Our water was turned off, and we had to use the neighbor's bathroom. We carried water from her house to ours to bathe and to ensure good hygiene for the girls at school. (Ms. Stella was an angel assigned to us). She prayed for me, shared the word of God, watched my children while I worked, and did so much more.

I was emotionally bankrupt, but I was still talking to God. I didn't understand walking in the fruits of the Spirit. I had a lot of hurts, but I still praised God. Tony was alive, but I was glad God slowed him down because he was walking all over me.

I packed up my family with just our clothes, climbed in our little green Saturn, and left town. I wiped the dust off my feet and never wanted to look back.

Mark 6:10-11, "He said, "Whatever house you enter, remain there until you leave that place. If a place doesn't welcome you or listen to you, as you leave, shake the dust off your feet as a witness against them." (CEB)

I relocated to my first apartment in Charlotte when I lived in the 'hood. The apartment manager graciously allowed me to return. I got my old job back at the hospital and felt blessed. I said to myself, "I got this!" I returned to my former church while Tony remained with his mother. He was upset because he felt like I had just left him. What he failed to realize what that it was too much wrestling with his mom. I understood he was her son, but she continued to blame me. Not to sound repetitive, but I was so drained, and my children were depressed.

I had peace as I started my life over with just my children. Of course, I worried about Tony, but I was at peace. God favored me that I never had a problem finding a job. It was just that I worked all the time and was still horrible at managing money. I knew I always had to pay my rent and lights, but can I keep it 110% real with you all? I found an agency that helped with rent and utilities, so sometimes I would spend my money on other things. I would go shopping, spend all my bill money on things for the house, clothes for the children, go to a movie, and eat out. I would overspend and think, "Okay, I have to go to Crisis Assistance Ministry!" They would help me each time I needed it, but as I matured in the Word of God, He told me I was abusing His grace and mercy. From then on, I started paying bills out of my paycheck.

I continued to work and care for my children, and we were doing fine. My husband and I were communicating, but we were not living together. He wanted to come home, but I was like, "What?" By that time, he was moving around well. He was talking and remembering things. All that was good, but I just didn't want to lose my peace. I was alone, smoking my sugar pebbles, and still tormented by thoughts of the past. They ran deep, and the devil loved to remind me that I was nothing. Unfortunately, those were the lies he had me believing.

As time passed, I did allow my husband to return home. We had no medication, proper education on brain injury, or anything to support his recovery. Tony was having seizures and was still using cocaine. After all the grace and mercy God bestowed upon him, he kept acting like he was the same Tony, but he wasn't the same Tony. He couldn't remember certain things or processes or even talk the same. His mobility wasn't the same either, especially in the mornings. I noticed, too, that he hated large crowds, and if we did walk past a crowd, he would move closer to me. To me, he was Tony, but he was deeply affected by the gunshot. He had post-traumatic stress disorder (PTSD), which emerged after a crushing and terrifying experience that involved physical damage. People who have PTSD can feel frightened even when they are not in danger. Tony still had temperament issues, but his anger level was more aggressive during that time. I also noticed that his words weren't processing out of his mouth. He couldn't tie his shoes, and lost many other everyday life skills, but his sex drive was very high. It was solid. As most brain injuries would decrease, very few develop hypersexuality, a rare but well-recognized sequela of brain injury. It has been defined as the subjective experience of losing control over sexuality.

    I used to pray for God to take Tony's desire away because he was ready when he emerged from his coma, and it was crazy. He used to curse before, but after the accident, he always cursed.

It was uncontrollable. People used to say he was playing me, but no. He didn't forget some things, but his outbursts and temperament were different. The brain is fragile, and if you're abusing drugs, that alters it even more, and many people are unaware of how this happens. So, I became nonchalant. They were talking but had no idea what I faced every day, day by day. To make matters worse, there were days when he didn't want to bathe and would forego one for almost a week. Things were terrible.

The side effects of frontal lobe injury are powerful, especially with one quickly becoming angry and frustrated, thinking children were out to get you. The mind alters from childhood to adulthood. There was no equilibrium, yet he refused to yield after all those years. It was 21 years, to be exact, with our anniversary each November. Tony chose to accept that he would never be the same.

Tony and I faced those challenges for years until he took a fall in August. He ended up being admitted to the hospital for a while. His doctors said he would not make it unless God restored him. Regardless of what they said, Tony came through everything they said he wouldn't. First and foremost, he's alive, and his mind works.

Antonio and Marsha Gonzales

CHAPTER 6

'TILL DEATH DO US PART

Tony's doctors said he would never be the same man I married because the damage to his brain was too severe. The frontal lobe function affected his memory, judgment, motor tasks, abstract thoughts, speaking, mood fluctuations, changes in social behavior, personality, and so much more. I was told he would never walk or talk, but he was doing all that and so much more. Tony was cutting grass, working on cars, and doing anything else he wanted to do. God has been so faithful to that man. He still has a call on his life despite his struggle with surrendering.

God also told me, "You're not in position! Your mouth is reckless as a woman of God!"

Proverbs 13:3, "Those who guard their lips

preserve their lives, but those who speak rashly will come to ruin." (NIV)

"You do not like to submit because you keep listening to the wrong people, and you haven't let things go from the past. I'm trying to do a new thing, and you're still holding on to the past."

I will be honest; I still wasn't walking upright concerning Tony because I was in the flesh. I felt like I was babysitting him. I had to help him a lot, and I couldn't help but think about the times when he cheated on me. But who did he need now? And he had cheated on me, but who did he need? I was angry and unforgiving of all the pain he had caused my children and me and how he allowed some of his friends and family members to treat me. They didn't do much in my presence, but in the conversations, he would share.

Matthew 6:14-15, "For if you forgive others

their trespasses, your heavenly Father will also forgive you, but if you do not forgive others, neither will your Father forgive your trespasses." (NRSV)

I was angry with God because I was still trying to be released, and I believed with everything in my heart, He was saying no. It wasn't long before my husband was sent to prison after being shot. He had pushed me, my son came from out of nowhere and punched him, and my daughter called the police. Tony was extradited to Texas and sentenced to prison for two years.

Antonio and Marsha Gonzales

CHAPTER 7

DONE THIS TIME FOR REAL

Well, days, weeks, months, and two years went by. During that time, I was battling with myself. I was raising teenagers, had addiction issues, a tormented mind, and 39 years of hurt. I constantly cried out to God but was slow in applying His word and gaining insight. I felt like He was giving me revelations in increments - a piece here and there. I was shifting, but it wasn't based on what I thought or wanted. I still was smoking and cursing and had an attitude out of this world, yet I still praised the Lord. I was begging Him to make me whole.

During Tony's and my separation, I remember I was so sick and tired that I called the prison to ask if they could tell my husband I forgave him forever and that I was tired of living.

After I hung up, it wasn't long before a deputy from the Mecklenburg County Sheriff's Department knocked on my door. I talked to myself for about thirty minutes. I'm still alive; glory to God. The next day Tony called, crying and apologizing. I received his certifications from Bible and parenting classes the following month. He asked to get paroled at my house, but I was knee-deep in drugs then. I was functioning but had to have a sugar pebble, smoke, and beer daily. My habit even increased from spending $10 to 20 dollars a day. I couldn't even get credit because my buddies didn't believe I smoked. The devil was trying to draw me in deeper and deeper, but the funny part about my addiction was that every time I got high, I would pray and read my Bible.

I needed my soul healed. I was broken. At that time, I was crying for God to help me! I told the Lord that I couldn't live like that and asked

Him to take all the pain and frustration away from me. I no longer felt like myself.

My husband called every day, but I still said no to him. I was not ready, so when it was time for him to be released, he went to stay with his sister. I visited him there, but I looked totally different than before. I was only weighing about 130 pounds and wore a size ten in clothes because the drugs were destroying me. Believe it or not, I liked my weight loss. I just felt like my face was just too skinny.

Psalm 118:8, "It is better to take refuge in the LORD than to trust in man." (ESV)

We talked and decided I needed time to myself. I was fighting, and he was trying to stay clean. It wasn't long before he fell back into the same cycle. There was no need for the both of us to drown, but I was fighting for my life. I struggled not to give up because I didn't want to destroy my children. I didn't want to hurt him, so I would go on dates and tell the men to separate their feelings and emotions. I made it clear that we were just kicking it. There were no strings attached. Granted, these were stable men with non-confrontational issues who knew how to stretch my mind with the word of God. My heart was broken, I loved my husband, but I enjoyed being wined, dined, and having fun. I looked out for myself because I was finally moving how I wanted to after being abused and mistreated. Nobody tried to control, isolate, or break me down mentally; I just wanted to be free from that bondage. I felt like I could breathe without walking on eggshells and was free from all the drama. It was also during that time when God showed me I was not responsible for another grown person's actions, but I was responsible for mine. Sadly, I failed to realize that my children were growing up in fear and trauma due to the circumstances they had been exposed to.

My heart started changing. I had a hard heart toward men, especially my husband. I even started hating my father because when I reached out for help, all I kept hearing from him was, "You're grown," or "I'm tired of hearing this!" I felt like I didn't have a home anymore; I was just out there in survival mode. Needless to say, God was holding on to me through all my mess. When I graduated from nursing class as a CNA 2 with a degree in Phlebotomy, God spoke to me clearly and said, "Don't you remember when you made it through school being on the honor roll? It wasn't your mom or dad; it's always been you and Me! Don't you think I got you?"

After several months, I decided to let Tony return home. God from Zion, why did I do that?

Antonio and Marsha Gonzales

CHAPTER 8

I LET HIM BACK

As time passed with Tony being home, we started attending church, but just going to church wasn't enough. When church ended, he and I would just begin arguing and fussing. He would talk down to me, say crazy things, and try to break me down. In turn, I would curse him out and yell at God. "How much longer? When will this end? If I haven't missed what You, why isn't the disrespect stopping?"

I just couldn't make sense of it all. Tony would hear the Word, come out of the church, wait until we got in the parking lot, and go in like a madman. What was so crazy was that he would start talking about events that happened five years ago. The devil was playing mind games with him, but it was as if he didn't hear anything about God, Jesus, or the Holy Spirit. I didn't make things any better because I fed right into it. I went back and forth with him instead of having a quiet spirit.

1 Peter 3:4, "You should clothe yourselves instead with the beauty that comes from within, the unfading beauty of a gentle and quiet spirit, which is so precious to God." (NLT)

One day, I was like, "Okay, God! I'm done! I don't want to be married anymore. I'm not cooking, washing clothes, having sex, or none of this. He can't respect me! F— him!"

I was still praising God, feeling His presence, and being blessed, but my mouth was sharp and deadly in many ways. Even my dad told me my mouth would make a man feel less than a man. Don't get me wrong, I was never proud of my mouth, but it is nothing like it used to be. God is doing extraordinary work in me. My daughter said something to me that had me thinking. She said, "Mom, how can you lead people if you can't listen to people and talk to us without going off?"

Proverbs 18:21. "Death and life are in the power of the tongue, And those who love it will eat its fruit." (NKJV)

Proverbs 15:1, "A soft answer turns away wrath, but a harsh word stirs up anger." (ESV)

God is still working on me because I also have a temper. I can jump, shout, speak in tongues, and still get mad. Conviction comes quickly if I fall short in those areas. Nevertheless, I give God so much praise because I was full of anger at one point and had no respect for anyone. My husband and I were two ticking bombs. We were very unhealthy and lacked self-control; for him, it's worse because he has a brain injury.

When Mr. Gonzalez was in prison, I hung out, had fun, and called myself living again. I picked up a sexual soul tie and momentarily let my emotions get the best of me. Beware that emotional ties are worse than sexual ties. Remember, Satan knows what we are longing for, such as conversations with sweet-sounding words. This person asked me to marry them, and we were just friends, but our discussions were always centered around God. My heart was just stuck on Mr. Gonzalez. When I say I was numb to men, I was numb, but when I let my guard down, I was drawn into that emotional soul tie and had to pull all the way back. I had to guard my heart so that my emotions wouldn't open doors for the enemy to trick me.

Proverbs 4:23, "Keep your heart with all diligence, For out of it spring the issues of life." (NKJV)

Those were some of the things my husband would throw up in my face, but it seemed as if he had forgotten about all the garbage he had in Saint Louis. I did not. I could only move past what happened when I began interceding for all those involved.

Matthew 5:43-44, "You have heard that it was said, 'You shall love your neighbor and hate your enemy.' But I say to you, Love your enemies and pray for those who persecute you." (NRSV)

I prayed for about two months to get over what Tony had done. I thought I was healed, but whenever the memories resurfaced, and I wanted to address them, God would say, "I thought you forgave him! And what did I tell you that I do with your sins once I've forgiven you? So why keep bringing it up?"

Micah 7:18-19, "Where is another God like you, who pardons the guilt of the remnant, overlooking the sins of his special people? You will not stay angry with your people forever, because you delight in showing unfailing love. Once again you will have compassion on us. You will trample our sins under your feet and throw them into the depths of the ocean!" (NLT)

Again, I ran to God, questioning Him about our broken marriage, how I could help others and my Garden of Gethsemane experience. He reminded me of what I asked Him for, "an anointing to love people like You, my Lord and Savior!"

I cried. "Why so much pain? Love is not pain! You, being Jesus, told me, "I chose you for this man because he can't have a weak-minded woman. He'll kill them verbally, and for where he's going, he will need you, and you will need him."

Then the Lord said, "You so worried about him; look at your insecure self. You won't be a good first lady if I bring him forward to his apostolic calling. For one, you're broken, mean, aggressive, hard-headed, unforgiven, hot-tempered, and you don't listen! You don't have enough word; just a hot mess."

"Look at yourself and ask God to help you; I got him!"

All I could do was look around the room, asking, "Did I hear this, or is this the enemy?" I was just wrestling with myself. The Holy Spirit checked me quickly, so I repented, got my journal out, and began talking to God about myself, especially my mouth. Truth be told, I was a mess. I would accuse my husband of everything, including if he were just being friendly and saying hello to someone. My mind would jump to accusations. "You talking to her?"

Things between us were a hot mess. Don't get me wrong, he did like the attention, especially since he was battling low self-esteem. And I didn't understand that. My husband was so sexy and had swag, mainly when he played pool before he got shot. He had a nice frame and was just a nice-looking man. In fact, he is still sexy to me.

After Tony got shot in the face, he never looked at himself in the mirror until about twelve years later. He was so self-conscious, always under me, but I thought he was just flirting. He was comfortable with me, and we were cool despite the toxic pain we'd caused each other. I also wasn't working well in that area myself; just broken was what I was. My husband always told me from day one that I was beautiful. "Don't you ever change, not even for me!" he would say. Ladies and gentlemen, I was so low in my self-esteem that every time I looked in the mirror, all I saw were my flaws. I saw my big nose, four children by four different men, and instability. (*At the time, things people said made me ashamed of my children. Now I know children are a blessing whether they came here the right way or not. God lent them to me, and I love them unconditionally. Do I condone bad behavior? No, nor do I make excuses for them or cover up for them. Accountability is essential.*)

I also felt ashamed of having a G.E.D. and being the first in Webster Groves to have a baby at 15. I fooled around with a family member's boyfriend, quit school despite being an honor roll student, had a cheating husband, was addicted to drugs, and the list went on and on. The devil was drilling one thing after another to keep me down.

Tony and I moved from state to state because we just couldn't decide where to settle down. He thought moving to a different state would stop the drugs, but that was not so. To my dismay, everywhere we went, he would find a hookup. Needless to say, we spent years traveling back and forth between the three states: Texas, North Carolina, and Missouri. God always had His hand on us; grace and mercy were always there.

Tony and I were often served eviction notices because we were poor money managers. No one taught us about the real world; it was like we learned through experiencing life. During those twenty-three years of being married, he and I learned a lot from one another, but one thing for sure is that we will never allow anyone to interfere in our marriage. We both call our parents from time to time, but my dad stays out of our marriage. On the other hand, my husband's mom will take his side, knowing he's wrong. All of his siblings say that Tony is his mom's favorite. Regardless, I don't want anybody interfering in our marriage unless God has handpicked them and sent them to us. The devil is clever, but please be careful who you talk to about your marriage.

My husband was so broken and wanted to be accepted that he would lie to his family to make me look bad. I can only guess he did so to go along with the shared conversations about our marriage. Because I had smoked crack and weed, his family thought I was horrible. They accused me of taking his money. I was appalled. *What money?* And I had to take the little bit he did have, or else the dope man would have our rent money. The same people putting their mouths on me forgot to check the mirror to see what they were doing. Sin is sin, and no sin is greater than the next. They forgot what they were doing and what I was doing; the only difference is that our choice of drugs was different.

Matthew 7:1-5, "Do not judge, so that you may not be judged. For with the judgment you make you will be judged, and the measure you give will be the measure you get. Why do you see the speck in your neighbor's eye, but do not notice the log in your own eye? Or how can you say to your neighbor, 'Let me take the speck out of your eye,' while the log is in your own eye? You hypocrite, first take the log out of your own eye, and then you will see clearly to take the speck out of your neighbor's eye." (NRSV)

God allowed Tony and my marriage to be displayed because He said He would get the glory. My husband is a man of many talents, even after being shot in the eye and with a bullet traveling through his head. He still does carpentry, mechanic, landscaping work, and much more. I call him Tony, the Tinker man. He will make it happen if we need something and I'm physically unable. If he had to scrape metal for my medicine, he has done it.

We have been in some low places, sleeping in our car, living in hotels, and staying with people. (I was thankful, but we made jokes with no disrespect to anyone. I would say, "Honey, I'm black! This isn't cool!) We lived in shelters where I was in a women's shelter, and he was in a men's shelter. We faced some incredibly hard times. We fought ourselves from within and tried to make progress but remained stuck for years. You may look at us now; we seem good, but behind closed doors and in the back of our minds, we are screaming for help.

I was drugged to numb the mess, but that took me deeper into the devil's den. My husband was used to masking things, but he'd been battling disappointment from his younger childhood, and so was I. After 23 years of marriage, I also learned that there were some things he lied to me about because he was ashamed. He failed to realize that I like him for being Tony and all that comes with him. He didn't know that he taught me some essential principles for life. No family is perfect; I know mine isn't, and you never know what happens behind closed doors. My husband taught me a lot. Marriage is not about material things like fancy cars, houses, clothes, or purses but about love and happiness, which can only come from Jesus.

I've been told that when I come around that I bring drama. Of course, I have drama if I'm dealing with myself, breaking cycles, and telling my dad several family members invaded me as a child. I'm drama. If I tell people you don't have to like my husband, I'm drama. Still, you're going to respect him because he was one that goes hard for my parents, children, grandchildren, brother, sister, cousin, uncle, aunt, and anyone else. I won't tolerate anyone saying what they want about him.

Genesis 2:24, "Therefore shall a man leave his father and his mother, and shall cleave unto his wife: and they shall be one flesh." (KJV)

I used to believe that until God started sharing with me, I was coming out of the cycle and breaking generational curses. Breaking generational curses causes a lot of things to transpire, and you know, when you confront things and expose the truth, people run from that. They call you a liar or a troublemaker. They deny things happen or just don't deal with it, avoid you, and avoid the conversation; it also makes the people involved have to deal with their mess. I also learned I had to deal with some deep-rooted things to be healed so I could move effectively.

Past situations can affect your adult life. For instance, if you've been touched the wrong way and are married, one touch can sometimes affect your sexual intimacy with your spouse. It has nothing to do with them, but your past can mess you up emotionally if not dealt with. I dealt with this after I stopped getting high. When you are high, it's a different kind of sexual encounter, but being sober and broken that's another sexual encounter. When God enters the picture, that's another encounter.

I was battling within. I deprived my husband just because of touch and memory. I was also coping with the past on whether to hold people accountable and whether their 'apology' frees you from the heavy baggage kept hidden and in secret, causing torment. This type of pain tempts you to do things that don't make sense. Even after my children grew up, I had to be accountable for the pain my life caused them, especially in my marriage. My husband tried to raise them but had no idea how to be a father. He was living a life of learned behavior, which was rough and not normal to me. We were different, but it was true when I said he did only what he knew with my children, and everybody doesn't have the same upbringing.

A lot of our fighting in our marriage came from jealousy. At one part in my marriage, my husband was jealous of my children. He always felt like I did too much or gave them their way. He also felt like they should have been doing many things that were too much for them regarding chores. We cleaned as a family, but he wanted them to work hard. I always told him these were my children, and I'm not Hispanic. In my culture, we don't make children work that hard. They were too young for that.

On the other hand, my husband had to work hard at a young age, and sometimes, he worked just to eat. He says his mom worked all the time, and even now, in her later years, she still works hard. I told Tony that if she stops working, she'll go down health-wise.

I always tell my husband that I admire his work ethic. He's a hard worker, and when he starts, he won't stop until he gets it done. People think he is slow because of his accident, but I tell people, "You better stop sleeping on my husband!" And I always tell my husband to stop sleeping on himself. That confidence is still not there all the way yet. Tony tries to prove his worth to himself, and he's no quitter. He works to defeat all odds. He has proved them wrong in almost everything people told me that Tony would never do. God's touch of love is amazing.

Before Tony, my children and I lived in Charlotte. They would visit their dads if they weren't in prison, spend time with my dad, or a lovely lady who's no longer alive, Anna Blackman, a jewel. (Sometimes strangers are better than family to a certain degree.) But my children were my reason for living. I needed them, and they needed me. At one point, I hurt my children by just exposing them to weed smoking, horrible language, disrespect from arguing in front of them and taking my frustration out on them. It was never physical abuse, but I was just snappy because I was going through it. I didn't stand up for myself; I either called the police or abandoned the relationship.

I didn't allow my husband to discipline my children. He thought everything a child did wrong was supposed to be disciplined. Well, I didn't feel that way. No, I didn't because I didn't get many spankings. I got some, but my husband always got spankings. He would call them *beatings*. Later, as God kept revealing things and peeling the layers off, my husband would open up about his childhood. Some things he told me were just not every day. I couldn't imagine someone I trusted handling me like that. But yet, not having a mom not take care of you is just as bad.

I love my mom, and all is forgiven and well. I was 47 when I realized that I was finally healed. So as my children matured into their late twenties, my girls shared that my husband had hit them for something they didn't do. I asked,

"Why did you wait until you grew up to tell me?" One said that she did tell me. The other one said she was scared. My husband doesn't remember, but they said it occurred twice. I did not play about anybody touching my children.

At one point, when I was arguing, I would keep to myself in my room, trying to hide the tears and keep the smell at bay. I was wrestling with my flesh and spirit, talking to God, getting high, reading the Bible, and listening to the gospel. I was begging God to take it away, take Tony away, and the drugs.

During my process of healing, I kept bringing up things to my dad from time to time. My dad told me he was sorry, but I blamed him repeatedly for my mom's mistakes while growing up. My dad was always there for me; I was 27 years old when he told me no for the first time. I was hurt because my dad never told me a lie. He told me he had to tell me no because I would have never grown up if he didn't. The only discipline I remember from my dad was when I stole 20 dollars from my Aunt Florence. It hurt so bad. Another time was when my dad smacked my face. I thought my face was coming off, and I wanted to kill him because I was that pissed. In my fifty years, I've only seen my dad angry four times but upset with me about five times, and this last time occurred when I was fifty years old.

My dad has never shown violence in front of me. I always remember my mom cutting on my daddy and cussing him out. I remember that he was bleeding everywhere. Despite it all, my dad never raised his voice, and I can never remember him raising his voice at me, but once when I told him, "F— u!" That's when he tried to run me over with his truck. Thank God for my grandmother and the truck not moving out of gear fast enough. As I got older, I learned my dad loved some women, and I remember a few other things I noticed as a little girl.

My husband loved to flirt. He was struggling, especially having one eye, speech problems, losing mobility in his hand, and other health issues. When he returned home, things were alright for a while. I was doing drugs, and he was out doing wrong. I know he was only mad because I was doing drugs and didn't share with him.

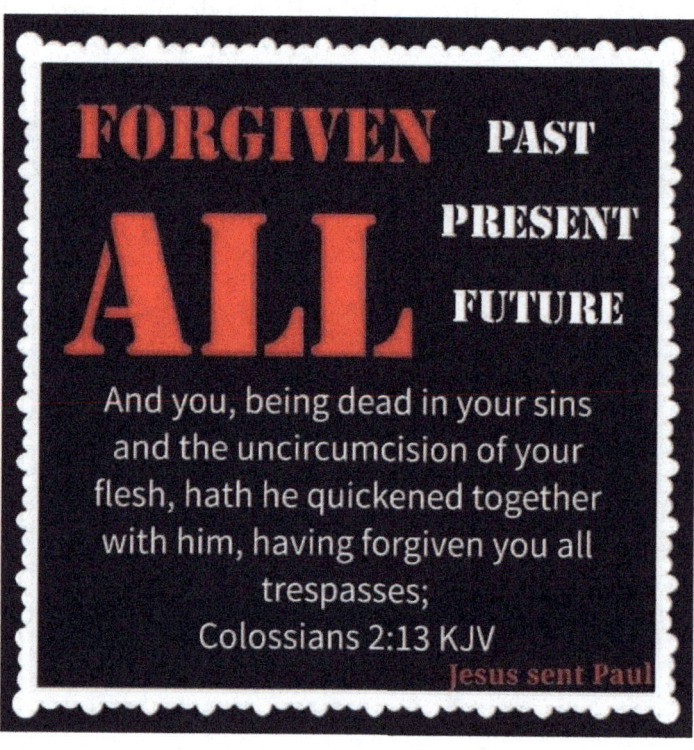

CHAPTER 9

ENOUGH IS ENOUGH

Mr. Gonzalez put his hand on me for the last time in 2010. It wasn't like he always fought me, but it happened, and it should have never happened. (Never stay in a domestic violence relationship.) I stayed with Tony because I was ordained to stay; it was only God, I believed it, and everything that happened confirmed that God was always in control. The protection alone was indescribable.

I divorced Mr. Gonzalez, and God said, "Let him back." I asked, "What? After all he did to me! I'm good!"

I was okay. I wasn't lonely, and I didn't want a relationship. I was dealing only with myself trying to heal. Tony was living with a lady who kept calling me, talking about all he did was talk about me. I was like, "Honey, I'm good! I don't miss him at all! You keep those problems!"

What I thought was strange was that I could still feel my husband. I knew when he was doing wrong and could feel his body's pain. I could taste his drugs on my tongue, yet we were not communicating. I kept telling God, "No, no! I don't want him!" I was fine.

One day, Tony popped up in Charlotte to visit. We hung out, and he handed me a ring, saying, "Will you marry me?" I said, "I really need to talk to God, but let's be friends!" I called my dad, who said to give Tony six months to see if he could stay clean. (When my husband was drug-free, he was like a big teddy bear. When he was high, he became paranoid for about ten hours straight, running around with a knife and accusing me of cheating. He would turn off lights, turn the blinds back and forth, talk about past events that never happened, and so much more. I had to pray to fall asleep and get some rest.)

I agreed to remarry Tony but didn't listen to my dad. We had a church wedding because, at that point, I was clean. I had no drugs in my system, no desire for them, and no side friends. I was good.

During the first few months, there was no looking back or temptation. Things were also cool regarding physical abuse though he would still get mad and quickly agitated over little things. I noticed his temper had worsened than before. He started abusing drugs every day instead of only on the weekends, and I became furious at myself. He was back into drugs, talking to me even worse than before, constantly angry and deeply saddened. I was like, "What's up with this dude?"

One day I worked on a traumatic brain injury (TBI) unit, and that's when it hit me. God said, "He has to see a doctor." I took Tony to the doctor because he was very depressed and had a lot of mood disorders. The doctor ran tests and examined him. We found out Tony had diabetes, and his medications weren't being monitored. The doctors then told me he had Dementia. "I'd like to meet this, Tony." I was used to all the behaviors and blow-ups. I also noticed things were different about him, but Tony refused to accept the doctor's negative words. I even saw his reading habits had changed. His right hand and right leg had nerve issues; the doctor said it would probably worsen. He sometimes had short-term memory loss, where he forgot phone numbers. He was going through a change.

The doctor ordered a CAT scan which revealed a small aneurysm. As I thought about it, Tony always had headaches but also a high pain tolerance. The pain could be kicking his behind, but he wouldn't tell me about it. I don't know how to explain this, but I can feel his pain when I am close to my husband. If he has a bad headache, sometimes I won't allow him to touch me because the symptoms transfer to me. It would no longer bother him but me; he would be the one with the headaches. When I pray for the headache pain to lift or cast off, it sometimes leaves quickly or might take a half hour.

Mark 16:17, "And these signs will accompany those who believe: in my name they will cast out demons; they will speak in new tongues." (ESV)

Tony would take his medicines when he wanted to. If he doesn't want to take it, he won't. And for some reason, he will not take his anti-seizure meds even when he knows what happens without them. By the grace of God, he hasn't had a seizure in a while.

I sometimes felt so angry with Tony because he did what he wanted, and so many people have died from the things he has survived. The doctors couldn't believe he had survived a headshot wound. They said only five percent of all victims survive gunshot wounds to the head. God had His hand on this man. He had been shot three times, three different times.

Matthew 22:14, "For many are called, but few are chosen." (KJV)

When I say my husband was Satan's tool, he would always get mad when I wanted to stay up and read the Bible. He would start cussing and trying to intimidate me. The Lord always reminded me that it was the spirits within him, not the person. All that warring and hardship I endured was training me to learn the spirit realm. I would tell my family that God was telling me to stay, and they would wonder, "God wouldn't do that!" Everybody told me that, but God would say, "What did I say? I told you, not them."

Numbers 23:19, "God is not a human being, that he should lie, or a mortal, that he should change his mind. Has he promised, and will he not do it? Has he spoken, and will he not fulfill it?" (NRSV)

God had to keep reassuring me that He chose me to walk through this ordeal. Did it get hard? Yes, life is hard sometimes, but if God ordained a thing, He knows how much pressure you can take and how long the process will take. I kept stopping on that journey. I wanted to give up, but God kept His hand on me every time I wandered. I was being broken for the rebuild. I couldn't bleed over people and lay my hands on them when I was all jacked up. My household can't be jacked up, and I'm trying to tell other people to do what's right. I was learning on so many levels to love God and myself, my husband, and my family the Godly way. I was learning the Word of God. I was learning to trust God and His Guidance. I was learning the ways of the Holy Spirit and so much more. I also learned about the devil and how he works. I am not glorifying him, just preparing to destroy his kingdom. Spirits are real, and I'm grateful for this journey. Even after twenty-three years, God still reveals things about my husband, children, and me.

First and foremost, we all need Jesus. He also reminded me to stop looking at people's marriages to desire what they have. God said, "Everything isn't what it appears to be." Now all marriages aren't jacked up; remember, nothing except Jesus Christ is perfect. God also told me. "You guys are breaking generational curses on so many levels." He also reminded me of the prayer I asked Him when I was first saved. I said, "Lord, I want an anointing like You to love people no matter what." I used to ask Him to feel what He felt. I also wanted to know why my husband acted the way he did. God said, "Be careful what you ask for." Marriage is work, and when you don't know the source of love, wait on God to teach you how to love him. Then you can love yourself more than others.

I have to be honest. My husband and I have personal struggles, but nothing we can't discuss and work through. With Christ, all things are possible. We pray together, we pray individually, and we pray with the family. We both have a relationship with Christ. We have grown so much collectively, together, and separately. My husband always wanted to speak English because he hated people's stereotypes about Latinos not knowing English. Yes, he would learn some words, but a few months into my marriage, God revealed that he didn't know what words meant because they could be slightly different from English to Spanish or vice versa. He would always take things the wrong way. That's why I always ask, "What does that mean?" I do that to ensure we're on the same page. He laughs when he speaks Spanish, and I translate what he says. He would say, "I thought you didn't know!" At one point, I didn't want to learn Tony's language because I hated my husband, and he felt the same way as we wrote this book.

Tony and I have had a chance to heal, but I still have to resolve some matters with my family. Is everything perfect? No, but my mother-in-law is getting along better now. I love her and never would disrespect her because I wasn't raised to do so, but if I had met her before the Lord came into my life, I would most likely not be married. I had no respect for my parents, so I knew I wouldn't have had any for his mom or any other adult.

I want to leave you with some Bible verses for strength.

1 Peter 5:10, "But the God of all grace, who hath called us unto his eternal glory by Christ Jesus, after that ye have suffered a while, make you perfect, stablish, strengthen, settle you." (KJV)

Galatians 6:9, "Let us not become weary in doing good, for at the proper time we will reap a harvest if we do not give up." (NIV)

Colossians 3:8, "But now you must also rid yourselves of all such things as these: anger, rage, malice, slander, and filthy language from your lips." (NIV)

Proverbs 6:32 says, "But a man who commits adultery has no sense; whoever does so destroys himself." (KJV)

Colossians 3:19, "Husbands, love your wives and do not be harsh with them." (NIV)

1 Corinthians 7:2-3, "But since sexual immorality is occurring, each man should have sexual relations with his own wife, and each woman with her own husband. The husband should fulfill his marital duty to his wife, and likewise the wife to her husband." (NIV)

Genesis 2:18, "The Lord God said, "It is not good for the man to be alone. I will make a helper suitable for him." (NIV)

Matthew 19:4-6, "Haven't you read," he replied, "that at the beginning the Creator 'made them male and female,' and said, 'For this reason a man will leave his father and mother and be united to his wife, and the two will become one flesh' So they are no longer two, but one flesh.

Therefore what God has joined together, let no one separate." (NIV)

Hebrews 13:4, "Marriage is to be honored by all, and husbands and wives must be faithful to each other. God will judge those who are immoral and those who commit adultery. (GNT)

Ecclesiastes 4:9-10, "Two are better off than one, because together they can work more effectively. If one of them falls down, the other can help him up. But if someone is alone and falls, it's just too bad, because there is no one to help him." (GNT)

I pray that everyone reads their Bible and remains in communion with God. I pray every married couple truly understands their vows as they stand before Christ. Ponder those vows and take them seriously. Blessings to you all.

Before closing out this book, I want to share an incident in March of 2021. I was working on a COVID floor, and I worked a lot. One day at work, I became so sick that I was weak, ill, and running a fever of 103.4. I told my supervisor I wasn't feeling good, and she said, "Marsha, you need to eat!" I wasn't feeling food or anything, so I began lying on the floors at work because the floors were cool. I was getting a little relief lying down, so I retook my temperature, entered my supervisor's office, threw it on her desk, and said, "I'm gone!" She said to call Employee Health and schedule a COVID test.

I drove an hour home and went into my room, and cried. I was sick. My husband rushed home and said, "Honey, I know you got COVID, but I know with all the problems in your health. I'm going to ask God to take it off you and let me carry it for you."

My husband prayed, and within ten minutes, I fell asleep. I didn't wake up until the following day. As I awoke, I noticed that I felt damp. I asked my husband if he had urinated on the bed, and he said, "Honey, I'm sick!" I cared for him all day.

I went in to get my COVID test, and the results returned negative. My husband went on the same day and was optimistic. He was so sick the first night. On the second night, my husband said, "Honey, we gotta go to the hospital!" I was terrified. He struggled to breathe, his sugar was uncontrollable, and his body ached terribly despite his high pain tolerance. Still, this time he couldn't shake it. God answered his prayer, and my husband said he would do it again for me.

My husband tells me, "I love you the only way I know how to," and it's been twelve years since he's touched me. Notwithstanding, that mouth on the both of us is being tamed by God, Himself. All glory belongs to God.

ABOUT THE AUTHOR

Antonio Gonzalez is from Victoria, Texas. He has seven sisters and five brothers. He also has one biological daughter, three stepdaughters, and one son. Antonia has four grandchildren, nieces and nephews, and great-nieces and nephews. He loves landscaping and carpentry work. Later in life, he looks forward to helping this young generation yield to the tug. He says his hands are yielding to his Creator.

Marsha Gonzalez is in nursing and sharing the gospel. She has a passion for helping difficult people, as society says. She feeds the homeless, hosts conferences to help empower the broken, and does prison ministry. She longs to do whatever God tells her to do. The two wrote this book to help enlighten couples about how critical it is to walk with God in any relationship.

Made in the USA
Columbia, SC
03 July 2023